Encouraging Words *for* Graduates

warnerpress

305800215238

Your Life Story

There has never been the slightest doubt in my mind that the God who started this great work in you would keep at it and bring it to a flourishing finish.

Philippians 1:6 (msg)

God is writing your story.

Often, the best stories are unpredictable—and the same holds true for the story of our lives. We might want the story to just sail happily from start to finish, but most of the time, that's not how God writes.

God weaves different characters in and out. The story may take a sad, scary, or difficult turn. But those very things lead to the most amazing happy endings.

Trust that God won't stop writing until your story is finished, and it's going to turn out great!

God Has a Plan

"For I know the plans I have for you," declares the Lord, "plans to prosper you and not to harm you, plans to give you hope and a future."

Jeremiah 29:11 (NIV)

Have you ever wondered what tomorrow might bring?

At one time or another, we all have. Sometimes the road we travel may be crooked and confusing. We may doubt the decisions we've made and wonder if we're doing the right thing.

When our path winds in directions that don't make sense, we can find comfort in knowing that God is in control. The Bible tells us that our life has been mapped out. When we trust God, we can be assured that although there may be twists and turns along the way, hope always waits around the corner.

LEARNING TO WAIT

When someone has been given much, much will be required in return; and when someone has been entrusted with much, even more will be required.

LUKE 12:48 (NLT)

We want God's answers to our prayers yesterday. Waiting on Him isn't even part of our mindset. We ask, God answers…immediately. Isn't that the way it works? Not exactly!

God isn't on our timetable. He sees things that need to happen during the waiting process to enable our growth and faith development. He knows how to bring about the result that He wants for our life. Our job is to be patient and allow Him to work.

Are you ready for the opportunities God has in store for you? Do you have the maturity, wisdom, and character to steward them well? Sometimes we find ourselves waiting on God to do something for us, but could it be that God is waiting for *us* to be ready?

Uniquely You!

We have different gifts,
according to the grace given to each of us.
Romans 12:6 (niv)

Have you ever gathered shells at the beach? Although you may find two that look alike, you will notice upon closer inspection that something about them is always different.

This is also true about us. People may appear similar in their outward appearance, their talents, or their personalities, yet we each have unique characteristics.

Our Creator made us for a special purpose, and His plan differs for everyone. By serving Him and using the gifts He has given us, we may best use our uniqueness for His glory.

Celebrate your God-given qualities today. You have been designed and chosen by God for a place in this world that only you can fill.

Don't Worry

Your heavenly Father already knows all your needs.
Seek the Kingdom of God above all else,
and live righteously, and he will give you everything
you need. So don't worry about tomorrow,
for tomorrow will bring its own worries.
Today's trouble is enough for today.

Matthew 6:32–34 (NLT)

How much time do we waste worrying about things that never happen?

Sleepless nights and high blood pressure are all we gain by worrying. Mentally repeating endless scenarios won't resolve our problems.

So, what is the solution? Lay your worries at the feet of Jesus and get a good night's sleep. Most things will seem much better in the morning.

Our Limitless God

With God all things are possible.

Matthew 19:26 (niv)

It's amazing to look up through the branches of a tall tree. A pine or redwood seems to rise to the heavens. Who would ever have thought that such a tall and mighty tree could grow from a tiny seed?

God can also take the small and simple things in our lives and transform them into towering successes. In Ephesians 3:20–21 (niv) we read, *Now to him who is able to do immeasurably more than all we ask or imagine, according to his power that is at work within us, to him be glory.* God can accomplish things we've never dreamed of or even considered. He is not limited by the size of our ideas.

No matter how big or small our hopes or dreams, we can trust them to our God who makes anything possible.

God Holds Your Future

I have told you these things, so that in me you may have peace. In this world you will have trouble. But take heart! I have overcome the world.

John 16:33 (niv)

Sometimes we think if we just plan carefully enough and think everything through, nothing bad will ever happen to us. That's just not true.

We live in an imperfect world, and no amount of human foresight can prevent trouble from coming. We can't and were never meant to depend on ourselves.

God wants us to rely on Him, not only in good times but in the bad times too. He is the only one who knows the future. We can trust Him.

Food for Thought

Whatever is true, whatever is noble,
whatever is right, whatever is pure, whatever is lovely,
whatever is admirable—if anything is excellent
or praiseworthy—think about such things.

Philippians 4:8 (niv)

We often hear the saying, "We are what we eat." So, too, we are what we think.

Jesus said that what comes out of our mouths comes from our hearts (Matthew 15:18). If we want to say forgiving, encouraging, loving things, we need those attributes within us. How can we meditate on good things when we are constantly bombarded with bad news? In today's world, can we realistically renew our minds and think thoughts that please God?

YES! We can counteract the world's thinking by reading God's Word. We can pray for guidance to understand and live by it. When we focus on God and His attributes—His plan, truth, love, and forgiveness—we'll have little room left for negative thoughts. Doing this consistently will change our attitudes, relationships, stress level, and our whole life!

Live for Jesus!

So if you're serious about living this new resurrection life with Christ, act like it. Pursue the things over which Christ presides. Don't shuffle along, eyes to the ground, absorbed with the things right in front of you. Look up, and be alert to what is going on around Christ—that's where the action is. See things from his perspective.

Colossians 3:1–2 (msg)

Do you know how we can outlast our short lives? By living with *eternity* in mind—by living for Jesus!

So many people have their minds set on earthly things. They are consumed with their jobs, relationships, and finances. All these are important, but they are temporary. If our priority in life centers on these things, we will be empty-handed when they are stripped away.

Those who focus on Jesus are never disappointed. Let's put the most effort into growing in our faith and sharing the good news with others. Let's live for what lasts forever.

When Storms Come

Never will I leave you; never will I forsake you.

Hebrews 13:5 (NIV)

Do you ever feel like you are all alone? Have you had times when the storms of life darkened your existence and clouds of turmoil left you feeling lost?

Although we sometimes may feel that life's problems are insurmountable, we don't need to face them alone. Our Creator says to each of us, "I am with you." His rock-solid promise assures us that no matter what we are going through, He will be there. Our circumstances don't cancel His closeness.

Storms may rage, but God's presence is unshakable. We can take comfort in knowing that our troubles won't last forever. With God's help, the clouds will part, and the sun will shine again. You are not alone.

God Is at Work

Trust God from the bottom of your heart;
don't try to figure out everything on your own.
Listen for God's voice in everything you do,
everywhere you go; he's the one
who will keep you on track.

Proverbs 3:5–6 (msg)

God wants to give you daily reminders that He is working behind the scenes in your life. Your responsibility is to be sensitive to His leading and to be on the lookout for His hand moving in your everyday circumstances.

Maybe someone will encourage you at just the right time. Or maybe you'll see a rainbow and realize God is reminding you of His promises. Maybe as you read your Bible, a verse will jump out at you and apply directly to your situation.

Be on the lookout for God moments today!

The Quality of Greatness

Whoever wants to become great among you must be your servant…just as the Son of Man did not come to be served, but to serve, and to give his life as a ransom for many.

Matthew 20:26–28 (NIV)

Many aspire to greatness, but few find it.

The quality of greatness is not found in wealth, fame, or leadership. Those who are truly great will not be found with crowns on their heads, but with towels around their waists.

They are the ones who have developed a servant's heart—always loving and living to bring joy to others. They are the ones who view their gifts and value their abilities as treasures from God—but who choose willingly to place others' interests and desires ahead of their own.

PERSISTENT PRAYERS

Keep on asking, and you will receive what you ask for. Keep on seeking, and you will find. Keep on knocking, and the door will be opened to you.

MATTHEW 7:7 (NLT)

Do you ever feel like you are annoying God by praying about certain situations daily?

God's Word reminds us of the importance of persistent prayer. We are far from being a bother to God. In fact, He invites us to communicate with Him as often as we want. The more the better!

So, when you are tempted to give up, quit praying, and think nothing is going to change, remember God hears, God cares, and you are not forgotten.

Planted with Purpose

Give thanks in all circumstances;
for this is God's will for you in Christ Jesus.
1 Thessalonians 5:18 (NIV)

For some of us, change is hard. We feel most secure in our familiar surroundings.

When God leads us to a new situation, we naturally resist being uprooted. We begin to act like finicky plants that have specific environmental requirements. We wonder: *Why isn't this "pot" like the last one? Why is this soil different from the dirt in my last "flower bed"? Why did I have to be transplanted in the first place?*

When those questions arise, tempting us to become nervous, we can reset our focus on all we have to be thankful for. Remember, a gardener always re-pots for the benefit of the plant—and that's what God does for us! When we think about it that way, it's easier to move forward with excitement and anticipation.

Facing Our Fears

The Lord is the strength of my life;
of whom shall I be afraid?

Psalm 27:1 (KJV)

Fear is a strange thing.

You might be surprised to learn how many people are afraid of birds…swallowing gum…clowns. We fear the unknown, change, or trying something new. Yet with God all our fears are needless. He will never leave us to face them on our own.

If we are constantly afraid, we will miss out on this amazing adventure called life. Let's trust God with our fears so we won't miss another minute!

God's Magnificent Love

The Lord *appeared to us in the past, saying:*
"I have loved you with an everlasting love;
I have drawn you with unfailing kindness."
Jeremiah 31:3 (NIV)

How can we grasp the extent of a limitless love?

We look into the sky and see the tops of trees or gaze upon a mountaintop with wonder. We see the stars and try to fathom their distance and the vastness of the universe as a whole. It is wider, deeper, and higher than we could ever imagine. So is God's magnificent love!

Are you discouraged? Have you lost someone you love? Do circumstances seem impossible? Do your sins seem beyond the scope of God's forgiveness? Remember, God's great love for you is more than a match for your most hopeless situation. His inexhaustible love covers absolutely every need.

Peace in the Valley

Peace I leave with you; my peace I give you....
Do not let your hearts be troubled
and do not be afraid.

John 14:27 (NIV)

We all experience valley times in our lives...seasons when life seems so hard, troubles come one after another, and challenges appear to loom over us. Often, our response is worry. As panic quickly sets in, anxiety threatens to overtake us.

But there is hope! We can find peace—a peace born of our faith in God. He is the One who created us, understands our deepest thoughts, and loves us unconditionally. Nothing we go through in this life is a surprise to Him. He cares and wants to support, encourage, and walk with us through every situation we face.

Willing to Learn

Teach me your way, Lord,
that I may rely on your faithfulness.
Psalm 86:11 (NIV)

Wouldn't it be wonderful if we could recapture the enthusiasm children have for learning? We were so excited about numbers, colors, and the alphabet. Building mansions from paper boxes and castles from wooden blocks kept us captivated for hours.

Jesus, our patient instructor, is still longing to teach us today—to give us the knowledge and wisdom we need to live. He wants us to live as little children, humbly accepting guidance and enthusiastically seeking truth.

Are we still willing to learn?

ARE YOU LISTENING?

Call to Me, and I will answer you. I will tell you of great things, things beyond what you can imagine, things you could never have known.

JEREMIAH 33:3 (VOICE)

When God speaks, you will know it!

Usually, you will have a very strong sense of a specific direction to take, or maybe a thought or idea that just won't go away. When you do something God doesn't want, you will feel uncomfortable in your soul. If you do, go in a different direction!

The time we spend in prayer and reading the Bible is never wasted. Often, that is when we hear God's voice most clearly. Let God lead you today.

Finding Your Purpose

Whatever your hand finds to do,
do it with all your might.
Ecclesiastes 9:10 (niv)

Did you ever stop to think about the purpose God has for your life? God has a plan for every person born.

One of the ways we recognize our purpose is through our desires: a carpenter wants to build, a teacher wants to teach, and a painter wants to paint. We accomplish what our Creator has planned for us by obtaining the tools we need to fulfill our dreams. Like a painter needs paint and a brush to paint a portrait or a fence, we need the proper tools such as a good education and strong work ethic.

Whatever we do, God wants us to give the best of our ability. How can you take the first step today? Ask God to help you find your purpose, and then do what God has created you to do.

Let God Lead

I know, Lord, that our lives are not our own.
We are not able to plan our own course.

Jeremiah 10:23 (NLT)

When was the last time you prayed about the direction of your life?

If we are honest, most of us pray, "Lord, let *my* will be done," not "Let *Your* will be done." We think we know the best way and the perfect solution. We presume to give the God of the universe our advice when it should be the other way around!

God is already working everything out, and He doesn't need our help. God may have a totally different plan than you do. Before you start stepping out and making decisions, pray they are from God. Trust Him with your concerns today.

GET IN THE BOAT!

Quiet! Be still!
MARK 4:39 (NIV)

Most people would like to live in a world filled with peace and tranquility—a place where life wouldn't "rock their boat." We try to create our own safe harbor by avoiding risky ventures or never leaving our comfort zone.

But God calls from the pier and tells us to launch out into the deep. He promises that He will be our safe harbor. Just as He calmed the wind and waves for His disciples, the Lord will do the same for us today.

So, get into your boat and do what God has called you to do. No matter what we encounter, we can be assured that God will restore peace to our lives when we anchor ourselves to Him.

Ready for Battle

No eye has seen, no ear has heard, and no mind has imagined what God has prepared for those who love him.

1 Corinthians 2:9 (NLT)

Times of trial reveal what we are made of. Some people crumple at the first sign of trouble. They are ready to retreat before the battle has even started! Other people rise up, form a plan, and prepare for what lies ahead.

God is using the challenges in your life right now to prepare you for victory in bigger battles in the future. As you *go* through some tough times, you will *grow* through them.

The decision is yours—retreat or rise up. Will God find you ready when it's time to fight?

Attention to Detail

Cast all your anxiety on him because he cares for you.

1 Peter 5:7 (niv)

Have you ever thought, *The list of my personal prayer concerns is so long…and I am only one of many. How can God possibly be interested in the details of my situation?*

God's ability to be everywhere at once and to know all things are attributes we can barely begin to understand. Just the fact that His great love causes Him to care is beyond us. Yet look at the attention to detail God gave as He fashioned a leaf…our bodies…the microscopic world we can't even see. The God who is aware of the death of each sparrow cares deeply about us!

If God cares about the smallest details of our world, we can trust that He cares about each of our concerns as well.

Stand Up for Jesus!

*If you do not stand firm in your faith,
you will not stand at all.*

Isaiah 7:9 (niv)

Have you experienced a situation where you need to stand and speak up?

Jesus didn't fit in. He did things differently than the leaders of His time. Though some people called Him crazy and some people called Him rebellious, God called Jesus His Son!

Jesus said that His followers would have to give up some things too. We might have to walk a path that leads away from what others are doing. It will be hard sometimes, and we may not understand why certain things happen. But if we follow Jesus' example, our lives will be better for it in the end.

No More Fear

There is no fear in love. But perfect love drives out fear.

1 John 4:18 (NIV)

Sometimes our fears can imprison us. We long for escape, for freedom. But the father of lies tries to ensnare us again with thoughts like: *What if I fail?* or *What if nobody likes me?* or *I'll never be good enough.* We are tempted to give in to defeat, and our God-given confidence slips away.

In times when fear overwhelms us, we must listen for God's voice. God will give us the strength and courage to do His will if we ask Him. God loves us unconditionally, and as His Word tells us, there is no fear in love.

God loves you, God believes in you, and through His grace, you are more than good enough. Claim that truth and find renewed courage today.

God Hears You

We live in the bold confidence that God hears our voices when we ask for things that fit His plan. And if we have no doubt that He hears our voices, we can be assured that He moves in response to our call.

1 John 5:14–15 (voice)

The enemy wants you to think your prayers aren't being heard and that God won't answer. But in Daniel 10:12 (ESV), we read, *From the first day...your words have been heard.*

The first day your mouth uttered the words, they were heard in heaven. The first time you prayed over your crisis, God heard you!

No matter how you feel or what your situation looks like right now—have faith. God hears your prayers.

Good, Clean Fun

Rejoice in the Lord always. I will say it again: Rejoice!

Philippians 4:4 (NIV)

Why do we sometimes think that even good, wholesome fun is less than spiritual? Maybe our tendency is to be immersed in so many "important" things that we feel guilty if we take time for rest and recreation.

We *need* innocent fun and laughter! The Bible tells us to rejoice. The simple joys of leisure can refresh us and foster this rejoicing, as we enjoy the good gifts God has given us. Without feeling guilty, we can spend time with our family, friends, or just by ourselves—knowing God wants us to!

God rested on the seventh day, setting an example for us. Let's follow His lead and take advantage of the time He's given us.

Do It Anyway!

Submit to God, and you will have peace;
then things will go well for you.

Job 22:21 (NLT)

No matter how silly it seems or crazy it sounds, you must listen to the voice of God and do whatever He says.

Sometimes in life, God will ask you to do something that doesn't make sense to you or anyone else. But when you know what that assignment is, just do it anyway. You will understand it later.

On the other side of your obedience and faith, a breakthrough and a miracle are waiting for you!

Even in the Shadows

Whoever dwells in the shelter of the Most High will rest in the shadow of the Almighty.

Psalm 91:1 (NIV)

Not every road God chooses for us is sunlit and pleasant. In fact, some places seem shadowed and forbidding. These paths test our faith. Can we find the strength to walk into the darkness, trusting God to guide and protect us?

We may be surprised to discover that the shadowed paths are actually under the wings of our Father, and the darkness is only the product of our own fear. That realization brings the opportunity to enter the presence of our Lord in an even deeper, more intimate way.

We need not fear where the Lord may lead us. We can trust His loving care, even in the shadows.

Knowing When to Surrender

I am glad to boast about my weaknesses,
so that the power of Christ can work through me.
That's why I take pleasure in my weaknesses,
and in the insults, hardships, persecutions,
and troubles that I suffer for Christ.
For when I am weak, then I am strong.

2 Corinthians 12:9–10 (NLT)

Surrendering a situation to God can be one of the hardest things we'll ever do.

Relinquishing control and admitting we can't do something in our own strength is humbling. No one wants to feel powerless.

But giving everything to God doesn't mean we are weaklings—it means we know the Source of all power and where our help comes from.

What We Do Matters

In everything set them an example
by doing what is good.
Titus 2:7 (NIV)

We usually make decisions based only on our personal circumstances. "It doesn't concern anyone else," we say. But is that really true?

Our actions often influence those around us. Our most far-reaching decisions could affect distant generations, like a raindrop that causes a pond's surface to ripple to the furthest edges of the water.

Think of the life of one specific Man, who influenced the world forever through His perfect love and sacrifice. As we consider the life of Jesus, may we be motivated to make our decisions not only for personal benefit, but for the good of society and the generations to come.

THE NARROW PATH

I am sure that our suffering now cannot be compared to the shining-greatness that He is going to give us.

ROMANS 8:18 (NLV)

Walking the narrow path is not easy.

Sometimes the way is steep. We trip on a root or stumble over a rock. Trees block the sun, and we think we aren't going to make it to the end of the journey. We question whether it would have been smarter to take the wider, easier path.

In those moments, God provides the encouragement we need to keep going. Continue doing the right thing. Focus on your goal and don't give up. God is with you.

The Light of God's Love

I am the light of the world.

John 8:12 (niv)

To a sailor, the lighthouse is a comforting sight. In the darkness of night, its steady beacon warns that the shoreline is nearby and to watch out for rocks and shallow water.

The lighthouse is also significant for Christians. It reminds us that Jesus is the Light of the world. As that Light, Jesus illuminates our path, leading us in the way we should go. In John 8:12 (niv) Jesus goes on to say, *Whoever follows me will never walk in darkness, but will have the light of life.*

That Light of life is the beacon that guides us. Our darkest trial cannot extinguish the light of God's love. We can move forward into the unknown without fear, trusting God will see us through.

WHERE HELP COMES FROM

*I lift up my eyes to the mountains—
where does my help come from? My help comes from
the LORD, the Maker of heaven and earth.*

PSALM 121:1–2 (NIV)

Where can you find solutions to your problems?

Your pastor and counselors, friends and family, self-help books, and TV programs can be good resources. But ultimately, our greatest source of help comes from the Lord.

Nothing can replace the hope, wisdom, and strength we gain from prayer and reading the Bible. It's never too late to begin!

WALK OF FAITH

Do not fear, for I am with you;
do not be dismayed, for I am your God.

ISAIAH 41:10 (NIV)

During our school days, we identified ourselves with our classmates. Their companionship added much to the joys and sorrows of our educational experience. Being part of the class provided a sense of belonging.

Now we may find ourselves floundering at times as we adjust to independence. We all must make one journey by ourselves—the walk of faith. We cannot hold anyone else responsible for the decisions we make on that trip; our choices are ours alone. But even in our solitude, God has provided for us by sending His Holy Spirit to live within us. A different, more important kind of learning takes place as we grow in wisdom through listening to His still, small voice.

Remember that God, your loving Companion, is beside and within you. He will guide you to His perfect will.

God's Record Book

You saw me before I was born.
Every day of my life was recorded in your book.
Every moment was laid out before
a single day had passed.

Psalm 139:16 (NLT)

God is keeping a record of every good deed you've ever done. He is keeping a record of every seed you have ever sown. You may think today that it went unnoticed, but God saw it. And in your time of need, He will make sure that somebody is there to help you!

GIVE IT TO GOD

Be still. Be patient. Expect the Eternal to arrive and set things right. Don't get upset when you see the worldly ones rising up the ladder. Don't be bothered by those who are anchored in wicked ways.

PSALM 37:7 (VOICE)

The Bible says we should do what the crisis requires and *having done all, to stand firm* (Ephesians 6:13, ESV). The word "stand" means to "abide or rest in God."

If you are trying to fix a situation today, stop right now and give it to God. Say, "Lord, this situation is too big for me. I can't change it or do what only You can do. I give You the weight of it. You have a plan, and I trust You with this circumstance!"

Momentary Troubles

For our light and momentary troubles are achieving for us an eternal glory that far outweighs them all.

2 Corinthians 4:17 (niv)

Struggles are temporary.

When we are facing a worrisome situation, we feel like the pain is never going to end. Fear and anxiety work overtime to immobilize us.

God understands our moments of weakness, but He doesn't want us to dwell there. His help is only a prayer away…morning, noon, or night. We can always call on Him.

Right on Time

Praise be to the Lord, who has given rest to his people Israel just as he promised. Not one word has failed of all the good promises he gave.

1 Kings 8:56 (NIV)

Life is full of surprises. We would like for all of them to be nice ones, and it can be nerve-wracking until we know for sure. We hope for a positive outcome and try to be patient, but it is so hard! We pray, wanting closure, and search God's Word for answers to our questions.

God is faithful, and what He has promised, He will do. You don't have to spend all your time wondering why God is, or is not, doing something. When you really trust God, you can be at peace knowing that at the right time, God *will* keep His promises.

It's going to happen, and the good news is, it's not going to be one second late!

Our Most Important Job

We should go up and take possession of the land,
for we can certainly do it.

Numbers 13:30 (NIV)

Our job in life is to obey God regardless of what others do. Part of living for Him means "going it alone" sometimes.

When God had Moses send twelve spies into the new land, ten of them said, "These people are too strong for us!" Two stood alone, confident that God would help them take the land. They eventually received the promise because they served a faithful God. And so do we!

Where is God leading you today? Are you exactly where you need to be? If you are feeling restless and worried, ask God if you are in the right place for this season in your life. Step away from wrong relationships, wrong jobs, wrong locations, and just watch what God had planned for you all along.

When Doors Close

Because of the Lord's great love we are not consumed, for his compassions never fail. They are new every morning; great is your faithfulness.

Lamentations 3:22–23 (NIV)

When we are experiencing an intense time, we can't help but ask, "Why, God?"

We know God is unfailingly good and kind. Our heartbreaking trials seem to fly in the face of all that He is. When we think we see the obvious, perfect solution, we can't understand the reasons why God wouldn't work things out the way we think He should.

Yet, we also know that out of some of life's greatest hardships come our greatest testimonies. God is faithful; God is merciful; God is all we need.

Making a Difference

Let us rejoice today and be glad.

Psalm 118:24 (niv)

Life is a gift best unwrapped slowly, but most days pass by in a blur. We become so busy we barely have time to catch a breath.

In times like these, we need God's gentle reminder to just slow down. Life isn't about how fast we accomplish our tasks. It's about the people we help and the memories we make along the way. Each day is filled with opportunities to make a difference in the world for God. We won't notice them if we are speeding along too quickly.

God has so many things to teach us, but He needs our time and attention. He wants us to draw close and focus on Him.

While You Are Waiting

If we must keep trusting God for something that hasn't happened yet, it teaches us to wait patiently and confidently. And in the same way— by our faith—the Holy Spirit helps us with our daily problems and in our praying.

Romans 8:25–26 (TLB)

Have you been waiting on God to do something that seems like it's never going to happen?

Sometimes the best things in life take a while, yet most people don't like to wait. If the wait seems too long in certain situations, you may be tempted to give up altogether, but please don't do that! Just because something hasn't happened yet does not mean it will never happen. The Bible says God will respond to us when the time is right.

God already has a certain date and time that He's planning on answering you! So why not just start enjoying your life with great anticipation and trust in His plan?

Find Your Prayer Partners

Therefore confess your sins to each other and pray for each other so that you may be healed. The prayer of a righteous person is powerful and effective.

James 5:16 (niv)

When we are experiencing a really hard time, just praying about it by ourselves may not be enough. We can become bogged down in discouragement and worry, and the temptation to give up is too strong.

God wants us to reach out and ask trusted people to pray with us. Their encouragement and faith may be just the boost we need to see a breakthrough.

In the Footsteps of Jesus

You make known to me the path of life;
you will fill me with joy in your presence,
with eternal pleasures at your right hand.

Psalm 16:11 (NIV)

How wonderful it is to know that Jesus journeys with us each day of our lives!

Jesus goes before us to clear a path so that we can follow in His footsteps. We never have to fear that Jesus will lose the way because He has made the journey before. He knows what it is like to be born and to live as a human being—even death holds no mystery for Him.

Even if we choose to ignore His guidance, Jesus doesn't abandon us. He patiently waits for us to acknowledge that we cannot find the way on our own and welcomes us back with love and forgiveness.

Let's follow Jesus and leave a trail of footprints for others seeking hope along the way.